MUSIC THROUGH TIME

PAUL HARRIS & SALLY ADAMS

FLUTE BOOK 3

CONTENTS

Music Department
OXFORD UNIVERSITY PRESS
Oxford and New York

The Italian astronomer Galileo was summoned before the Papal Inquisition for his support of the blasphemous theory that the earth revolved around the sun—the Church decreed that it was the other way round. The next year he was banned from doing any scientific work.

Praetorius compiled a set of dances for the Duke of Brunswick which he called *Terpsichore* after the Greek Muse of dancing. This piece is one of the movements from that collection.

1615
Courante

Michael Praetorius
(1571–1621)

1716
Les Roseaux

François Couperin
(1688–1733)

The piano, invented around 1700, was becoming increasingly popular at this time—it had a greater dynamic range than the harpsichord, partly because the strings were struck by hammers and not plucked.

Couperin published a book on the art of keyboard playing in this year. Most of his pieces have descriptive titles such as this one, 'The Reeds', which is an arrangement of a harpsichord piece.

5

1729
Bourrée

J. S. Bach, the other great composer of the Baroque period, composed his *St Matthew Passion*. It was first performed on 15 April this year.

George Frideric Handel
(1685–1759)

The bourrée is a lively dance which originated in France.

1760
Menuetto

William Boyce
(1710–79)

The first roller-skate was designed by the Belgian Jean-Joseph Merlin, but turned out to be a disaster when demonstrated. The four-wheeled versions in use today weren't patented until over a hundred years later, in 1863. The famous Royal Botanical Gardens were opened at Kew in London.

William Boyce spent many years in charge of King George III's orchestra. Like Beethoven, he became deaf in later life. This Menuetto is from his third symphony.

1777
Theme and Variation

Wolfgang Amadeus Mozart
(1756–91)

Following the American declaration of independence from Britain in the previous year, the two countries went to war. Independence was formally agreed in 1783. The 'Stars and Stripes' was the new American flag: initially it had only thirteen stars, representing the thirteen American colonies.

Mozart wrote four flute quartets. This melody is taken from the second, and he later used it in his Serenade for thirteen wind instruments.

The metric system was adopted in France. It was based on the standard length of a metre, defined as one ten-millionth of the distance from the North Pole to the Equator. The first horse-drawn railroad appeared in England.

Danzi was one of the first composers to write for wind quintet (flute, oboe, clarinet, horn, and bassoon). He also composed two flute concertos; this Larghetto is from the first.

Larghetto

Franz Danzi
(1763–1826)

1823
Menuetto and Trio

Franz Schubert
(1797–1828)

Charles Macintosh developed a new fabric used for making raincoats. Though waterproof, the material was found to give off a strong smell in the summer heat. William Webb Ellis, a boy at Rugby school, broke the rules of football, unwittingly starting the development of a new game known as 'rugby'.

Although he died young, Schubert wrote a great amount of music during his short life including many short dance movements for the piano. This piece is an arrangement of one of them.

1861
The Christmas Tree

Niels Gade
(1817–90)

Civil war broke out in America between seven Southern Confederate States and the Northern Union. The defeat of the South two years later led to the abolition of slavery. In England, daily weather forecasts began and the first horse-drawn trams appeared in London.

Niels Gade was a Danish composer. He wrote eight symphonies, as well as many piano pieces.

16

17

1889
Allegretto

Antonin Dvořák
(1841–1904)

The 1,000-foot Eiffel Tower was built in a few months for the Paris Centennial Exposition. The designer and engineer, Alexandre Gustave Eiffel (who had also designed the inner structure of the Statue of Liberty in New York, four years earlier), received the profits from the tower for the following twenty years.

Dvořák's music was strongly influenced by the folk-music of his native Czechoslovakia. This Allegretto appears in the second movement of his eighth symphony.

19

1889
Dance a Cachucha

Arthur Sullivan
(1842–1900)

Coca-Cola first appeared in Atlanta, claiming to cure everything from the common cold to hysteria! In London, over 10, 000 dockers went on strike; after a month, their demands were met—a salary of sixpence an hour.

The Cachucha is an Andalusian dance. This one appears in *The Gondoliers*, a comic opera by Gilbert and Sullivan which is set in Venice.

22

1891
Norwegian Melody

The Prince of Wales caused a scandal by appearing as a witness in a libel case about cheating at cards. The first ten-storey 'skyscraper' appeared in Boston. Work started on the Trans-Siberian railway in Russia. Arthur Conan Doyle wrote *The Adventures of Sherlock Holmes*.

Grieg was influenced by the music of his Norwegian homeland. Perhaps his most famous piece is the Piano Concerto in A minor, with its distinctive opening chords.

Edvard Grieg
(1843–1907)

Arietta

Samuil Maikapar
(1867–1916)

Karl Benz in Germany and Henry Ford in the USA
built their first motor cars. Alexander Graham Bell
made the first long-distance telephone call,
from Chicago to New York.

Samuil Maikapar was a professor at the St Petersburg
Conservatory in Russia. He wrote many pieces for
piano and this is an arrangement of one of them.

1911
Marie Antoinette

Scott Joplin
(1868–1917)

Marie Curie was awarded the Nobel Prize—her second—for her work on radioactivity. Her death from leukemia 23 years later was caused by the dangerous chemicals she handled. In Britain, the Official Secrets Act became law, making certain areas of Government work secret in the interests of national security.

Scott Joplin was the major figure in the history of Ragtime—an early type of jazz featuring syncopated rhythms.

1940
The Music Lesson

William Walton
(1902–83)

Hitler invaded Norway, The Netherlands, Belgium, and France. The Blitz left London badly damaged and Winston Churchill became Prime Minister of a coalition government in Britain. Stalin's rival, Leon Trotsky, was assassinated with an ice-pick in Mexico City.

Walton became famous after he composed *Façade* , a work for reciter and small ensemble which included elements of jazz. He later wrote two symphonies, three concertos, and music for several films.

30

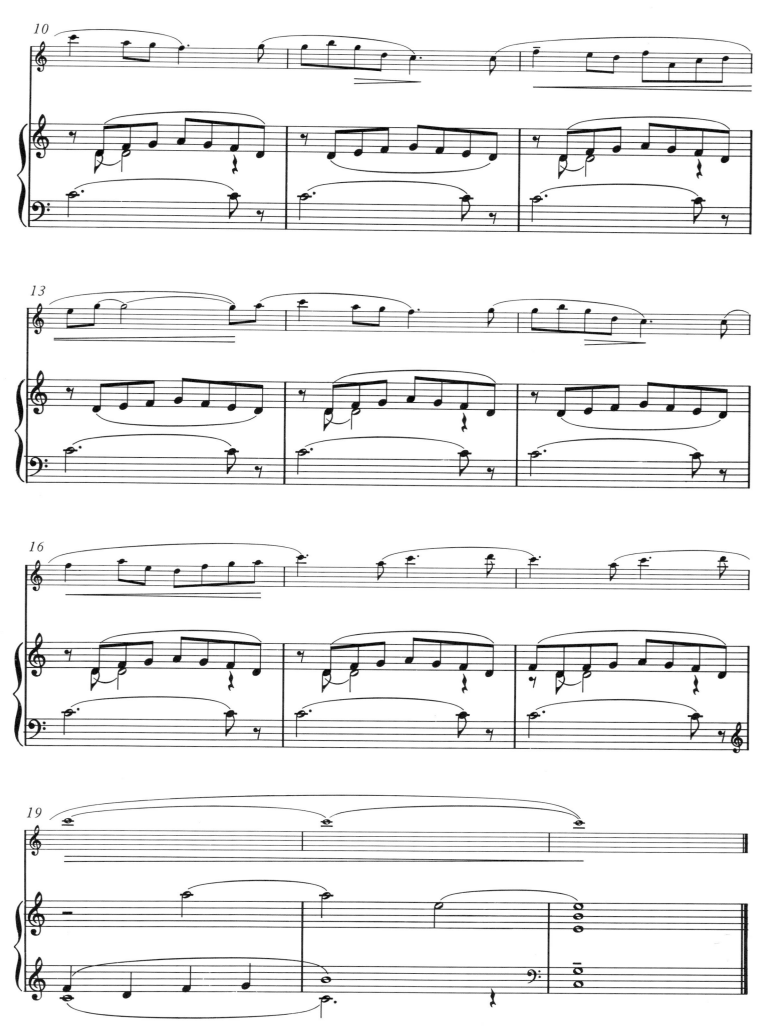

31

1950
Air

Robin Milford
(1903–59)

China, which had become a Communist State the previous year, invaded Tibet. The Korean Civil War began and India became an Independent Republic under Prime Minister Nehru. Frank Loesser's musical *Guys and Dolls* was produced on Broadway in New York.

Robin Milford was a pupil of Holst and Vaughan Williams. Many of his pieces are still unpublished and can be found in the Bodleian Library in Oxford.

1990
Caprice Français

This is a highly spirited piece, full of the hustle and bustle of busy Parisian boulevards! It should be played in a jaunty manner, with a great deal of joie de vivre.

Paul Harris
(1957–   )

35

Reproduced and printed by
Halstan & Co. Ltd., Amersham, Bucks., England